IS THAT WHAT YOU MEAN?

Paul Hancock

PENGUIN ENGLISH

PENGUIN BOOKS

Published by the Penguin Group
Penguin Books Ltd, 27 Wrights Lane, London W8 5TZ, England
Viking Penguin, a division of Penguin Books USA Inc.
375 Hudson Street, New York, New York 10014, USA
Penguin Books Australia Ltd, Ringwood, Victoria, Australia
Penguin Books Canada Ltd, 2801 John Street, Markham, Ontario, Canada L3R 1B4
Penguin Books (NZ) Ltd, 182–190 Wairau Road, Auckland 10, New Zealand

Penguin Books Ltd, Registered Offices: Harmondsworth, Middlesex, England

First published 1990
10 9 8 7 6 5 4 3 2 1

Designed by DW Design Partnership Ltd
Illustrations by Clive Collins

Printed in England by Clays Ltd, St Ives plc

CONTENTS

INTRODUCTION

To the Student

Everybody makes mistakes when they learn a language and everybody wants to correct them as much as possible. This is difficult if you do not understand *why* something is wrong. *Is That What You Mean?* will help you to understand why a mistake is wrong and help you to correct it.

This is the best way to use each unit of this book:
1. Look at the pictures and explanations and correct the mistakes.
2. Look at the answers in the back of the book to check that your answers are correct.
3. Do the first practice exercise A. Look again at the pictures and explanations if you are not sure if the practice sentences are right or wrong. Correct the sentences which are wrong.
4. Check your answers to exercise A in the back of the book.
5. Do the practice exercise B. Look at the pictures and explanations again if you are not sure what to write.
6. Check your answers.

To the Teacher

This book can be used in a General English class or an extra grammar class, with students who are at Intermediate level. Lower Intermediate students will be able to use the book but may need more help from you. It is very easy to use and will help all students to see why some of the common mistakes they make are wrong, and give them practice in error correction which is both effective and enjoyable. Each unit deals with a variety of errors, covering tenses, other grammatical points (e.g. articles), confused words and prepositions. There is an answer key at the back of the book.

How to use each unit of the book in class:

1. Put the students in pairs or groups. Ask them to look at the pictures and explanations and correct the mistakes.
2. When they have finished, check the corrections as a class. Ask the students to explain again why the first sentence was wrong.
3. Ask them to do the first practice exercise A in pairs or groups. You could teach or check any vocabulary which your class might not know. You can go round and help any students who are having problems by referring them to the relevant picture and explanation.
4. Check the answers as a class and make sure that they understand why each sentence was right or wrong, and why the mistakes are funny.
5. Ask them to do the gap-fill exercise in pairs or groups. Again, you could teach or check vocabulary if necessary before they do the exercise, and help any students who are having problems. This exercise could also be done for homework, or in a later lesson for revision.
6. Check the answers in class.

The pictures and explanations are useful to refer back to if students make any of these mistakes in later classes or in their homework.

1

'Try to phone Michael – he might be at home.'

If you use *try* with the infinitive, it means that the action is something difficult and you have to try very hard because you might not be able to do it:
e.g. 'Try to walk' (your leg is injured);
'Try to sleep' (there's a lot of noise in the house).

'Try .... Michael – he might be at home.'

Here you need to use *try* with the verb in another form, so that it means *experiment*. It's not a difficult thing to do – you just do it and wait to see what the result is.

2

**'There were very little people in the
supermarket this morning.'**

Little is the opposite of *much*, and is used with
uncountable nouns e.g. 'I have very little time.' If you use
little with a plural noun, it means *small*,
e.g. 'There were some beautiful little houses near the beach.'

'There were very .... people in the supermarket this morning.'

People is a plural noun, e.g. 'The people are friendly here.' With a plural noun you have to use a different word, which means the opposite of 'many'.

3

'After the bell rang, the boxers continued hitting themselves.'

The reflexive pronoun *themselves* means that one person is doing something to himself or herself, and the other person is doing something to himself or herself. This is used for sentences such as 'The children washed themselves and got into bed.'

'After the bell rang, the boxers continued
hitting ....'

If both people are doing something to the other person, you use
two words.

4

**'Unfortunately the coffee machine is out
of work.'**

Only a person can be *out of work*, because it means
without a job, or *unemployed*,
e.g. 'In Britain there were nearly 3 million people out of
work in the 1980s.'

'Unfortunately the coffee machine is out
of ....'

For a machine which isn't working because it is broken, you
need another word instead of *work*.

5

**'Three men stole a bank in North London
yesterday.'**

You can only steal things that you can move, because if you
steal something, you take it away from the place or person it
belongs to,
e.g. 'She stole some money from the cash box.'

**'Three men .... a bank
in North London yesterday.'**

If you talk about the place that people steal things from, you
use a different verb.

6

**'The ticket inspector came into the
compartment and controlled our tickets.'**

If you *control* something, it means that you have power over
it and can make it do what you want,
e.g. 'The government controls the country', 'The driver couldn't
control his car and it went off the road.'

'The ticket inspector came into the
compartment and .... our tickets.'

When you enter Britain you can see a sign saying
Passport Control, but you can't say that the Passport
officials *control your passport*. Here you need the verb
that means *to examine and look for any mistakes*.

'My landlady is a very good cooker.'

A teacher teaches, and a writer writes, but a *cooker* is not the person who cooks. A cooker is a machine which cooks, just as a dishwasher is a machine which washes dishes.

'My landlady is a very good ....'

For the person who cooks, you just use the verb as a noun.

8

'They hoped the firemen would arrive on time.'

If you do something *on* time, you do it punctually, at exactly the time that was arranged before,
e.g. 'Because so many people go on holiday, not many planes take off on time these days.'

**'They hoped the firemen would
arrive .... time.'**

Here you need a different preposition with *time* to mean
early enough. In a difficult or dangerous situation like this,
it means *early enough to stop something bad happening*.
It can also mean *before* a time which was arranged previously.

9

**'Nick couldn't reach the hammer, so he
asked Bob to throw it at him.'**

As well as *throw*, there are some other verbs like *shout*
and *point*, which have a different meaning with different
prepositions. If you use them with *at*, it means you do the
action in an angry and unfriendly way,
e.g. 'I know I made a mistake, but you don't have to shout at me.'

'Nick couldn't reach the hammer, so he
asked Bob to throw it .... him.'

If someone does these actions in a friendly, helpful way, you
use a different preposition.

10

'Philippa usually goes to work with her car.'

If you went somewhere *with* your car, it would be the same as
going with another person,
i.e. it would accompany you.

'Philippa usually goes to work ....'

If you prefer to sit inside your car when you're travelling,
use a different preposition. Also, you just use *car*, without
her or *my* etc.

PRACTICE

UNIT ONE

 Decide whether the following sentences are right or wrong. If a sentence is wrong, correct it.

1. When Jakob realized he was locked out of the house, he tried to knock on the door.
2. If you have a headache, try taking an aspirin.
3. I lost my watch on the beach and three of my friends tried finding it for me.
4. Mick and Sarah often meet themselves in the town centre.
5. Paul and Colin are both good at tennis so they enjoy playing each other.
6. I'm afraid there is very little food in the house.
7. There was a lot of trouble at the football match because there were very little policemen there.
8. Now that we have a drinks machine the coffee lady will be out of work.
9. We had to carry our bags upstairs because the lift was out of work.
10. Our telephone is out of order, so you'll have to use the neighbour's.
11. Stuart told me that the Post Office in Chinnor was stolen last week.
12. The new bank in Geneva is impossible to rob.
13. Sometimes Miss Kavanagh's students were very difficult to control.
14. The man at the US embassy checked our passports and gave us a visa.
15. Every time I arrive in England the customs men control my luggage.
16. Julie doesn't like washing up – she prefers to be the cooker.
17. After Joan has made a big meal John usually has to clean the cooker.
18. The trains in Greece never arrive in time.
19. The hotel bathroom flooded because Vicki didn't turn the taps off on time.
20. If the play starts on time we should be able to get out of the theatre in time to catch the last train home.
21. Harriet took a photograph of Robert throwing the doll at his little sister.
22. Karen was so angry with Keith that she threw her tennis racket to him.
23. Martin saw his brother on the other side of the street and shouted to him.
24. Sue's car is being repaired, so she's going to come with her bicycle.
25. The cinema is very near here, so you don't need to go by your car.

B *Complete the following text, using one of the words or phrases you have practised in this unit:*

I had decided to go into town (1) .... car, hoping that it would be easy to find a free parking place. The streets were full of cars, even though there seemed to be (2) .... people in the town centre, and so I had to go to a car park. I found the ticket machine, but it was out (3) ....

I didn't want to leave the car without a ticket because York is full of bored traffic wardens, who (4) .... all the cars to make sure that the owners have paid. I think it's probably easier to (5) .... a bank than park your car without paying! I tried (find) (6) .... a traffic warden so that I could explain my problem, but of course, you can never find one if you want to! I had very (7) .... time, so in the end I decided to leave some money on top of the car and hope that no one would (8) .... it.

It was 2.00 p.m. by now, and I had arranged to meet my friend Alastair in an Indian restaurant at 1.45 p.m., so I hoped he hadn't arrived (9) .... time. I tried (phone) (10) .... the restaurant to let him know that I would be late. One of the (11) .... who worked in the restaurant kitchen answered the phone, but he said he couldn't see anyone in the restaurant who looked like Alastair.

When I got to the restaurant, Alastair wasn't there yet. I was standing next to two men, who were having an argument at the bar. One of them threw his drink (12) .... the other and I thought they were going to start hitting (13) ...., but the manager came over (14) .... time to stop them.

As the manager was throwing them out, I saw Alastair standing in the doorway, looking for me. I shouted (15) .... him, and once the waiter had brought us our food and drinks, I finally began to relax.

1

'I wish you would be taller.'

If you wish someone *would/would not* do or be something, it must
be something that it is *possible* for them to change. It can make you
angry that they don't change,
e.g. 'I wish you would speak more slowly.'

'I wish you .... taller.'

If it is something that it is impossible to change, e.g. a person's face or height, you are making an impossible wish; therefore use a past tense (here the Simple Past).

2

**'At work today, my boss told me that I
must stop to sleep.'**

If you stop to sleep it means that you stop what you are doing
in order to sleep,
e.g. 'When I was walking home, I stopped to buy a newspaper'
(I stopped walking to buy a newspaper).

'At work today, my boss told me that I
must stop ....'

For the action that you stop, you need to use the verb in
another form, and not the infinitive.

3

'I am very boring in this class.'

If someone or something is bor*ing*, it is causing the problem.
You do not usually tell people that *you* are boring! You might
say that a *lesson* is boring (or exciting).

'I'm very .... in this class.'

Here you are describing how you feel when you think another thing is boring.

4

BIRMINGHAM NEW STREET

**'Jack had to change the train in
Birmingham.'**

The meaning of change in this sentence is *to make it different*,
e.g. 'You've changed your hair' (it is a different style or colour).

'Jack had to change ....
in Birmingham.'

If you get out of one train and get into another one, you have to talk about more than one train. Also, you don't use *the*.

5

**'My mother spilt coffee on my dress so
that I had to wear a different one.'**

If you use *so that* without a comma before it, it tells you
the reason *why* you do something,
e.g. 'I closed the curtain so that I could sleep.' It means
that you *wanted* the second thing to happen.

**'My mother spilt coffee on my dress ....
I had to wear a different one.'**

Here something happens as a result of an action, but nobody
wanted it to happen. Use only one word, and put a comma before it.

6

**'Your plants have grown up a lot
since my last visit.'**

People grow up, when they get older and stop *behaving* like children. When you grow up you start to do adult things.

'Your plants have .... a lot
since my last visit.'

Here you are talking about something getting bigger. You don't
need a preposition for this.

7

**'Parents should educate their children
more strictly.'**

In English, *education* is something that happens in schools.
Teachers educate children by giving them lessons about
different subjects.

'Parents should .... their children .... more strictly.'

Few parents educate their children themselves. Parents look after their children and show them how to behave. Use a phrasal verb here. *Their children* comes between the two parts of the verb.

8

**'It's nice to go on holiday and be
completely careless.'**

If you are *careless* it means that you do not pay attention to
what you are doing, so you make mistakes or have accidents.

**'It's nice to go on holiday and be
completely ....'**

If you want to say that you have no worries or responsibilities,
you use the word *care* to make a different adjective.

9

**'After two hours, the train arrived on
the platform.'**

People *stand on* the platform while they are waiting for the
train. If the train is *on* the platform you have a disaster.

'After two hours, the train arrived ....
the platform.'

Use one of the other prepositions you can use with *arrive*
(*to* is *not* one of them!).

'My uncle Tom died with pneumonia.'

It's possible to die with another person (or with your dog!).
It means that you both die at the same time.

'My uncle Tom died .... pneumonia.'

You die *from* things which come from outside,
e.g. from an injury, but you use a different preposition for
illnesses which start inside you.

PRACTICE

UNIT TWO

 Decide whether the following sentences are right or wrong. If a sentence is wrong, correct it.

1. Dan wishes Joanna would spend less time in the bathroom.
2. Don't you wish I would have blue eyes?
3. Diana's friend wishes she played her music more quietly.
4. I wish I didn't have three brothers.
5. Fiona stopped to smoke three years ago.
6. I saw Amanda when I was walking in the park, but we didn't stop to talk.
7. I don't speak English very well. I stopped to learn it when I was fifteen.
8. Tim left before the film finished because he was boring.
9. I'm very exciting about my new job, because it's never boring.
10. Because Benedicte didn't like the view from the balcony, Steve asked if they could change the room.
11. It's cheaper to fly from Paris, but you have to change planes three times.
12. The sun shone for five days so that Katie got very brown.
13. The car ran out of petrol so that we had to walk to the hotel.
14. The hotel was expensive, so Inge decided to find another one.
15. My dog has grown up so much he can jump into the next garden now.
16. Clare, you're behaving like a baby – why don't you grow up?
17. The tree you bought is growing very quickly – it will probably have apples on it next year.
18. Christine's children are very well-educated. They never take things without asking.
19. It's not easy for both parents to work and bring children up.
20. My parents educated me very well and I went to a very good school.
21. Miles would like to be young and careless again.
22. You speak English very well, but you are too careless with your written work.
23. There were hundreds of people waiting at the platform when the train arrived.
24. The Prime Minister suddenly died with a heart attack.
25. Five people died from their injuries when a bus crashed yesterday.

B *Complete the following text, using one of the words or phrases you have practised in this unit:*

Richard Rogers wanted to catch the 8.30 train to Reading. Unfortunately his alarm clock didn't work, (1) .... he had to catch the 9.15 train. Now he was standing (2) .... the platform at Reading station, where he had to change (3) .... The train was already twenty minutes late.

'I wish the train (come) (4) ....,' he said to himself. At last the train stopped (5) .... the platform and he found a seat. Unfortunately he was sitting next to some very badly behaved children, who were making a lot of noise. Their parents kept telling them to be quiet, but they wouldn't stop (shout) (6) .... and (hit) (7) .... each other.

'When I have children I'll (8) .... them .... quite strictly,' Richard thought. His father had died (9) .... a heart attack when Richard was six, but his mother had been very firm with him as a child, and he had (10) .... to become a man who liked discipline and hard work.

'I wish Gatwick Airport (11) .... closer to London,' he thought, as the train stopped (let) (12) .... more people on at another station. At last he arrived at Gatwick, and was soon waiting to get on the plane to Italy. He bought a book from the bookshop (13) .... he would have something to read if the plane was late taking off. When he was younger he used to find flying exciting, but because he often flew on business now, he usually felt very (14) .... on aeroplanes. But he was already looking forward to forgetting all about work, eating good Italian food, lying on the beach, and feeling completely (15) ....

1

'I have been smoking thirty cigarettes today.'

If you use the Present Perfect Continuous, it means that the same action (smoking thirty cigarettes at the same time) has continued over *a period of time*. You can say 'I've been smoking today' or 'I've been teaching twenty students all day'.

'I've .... thirty
cigarettes today.'

Here, what is important is not the period of time an action
has continued for, but *how many* cigarettes were smoked as
a result. To talk about the result, you don't use the
continuous form.

2

**'After putting on my new dress, my husband
told me that the taxi had arrived.'**

You can join two actions using *after* + *...ing*, but only if the
same person does both the actions,
e.g. 'After having a shower, my husband went out.' This means
'My husband had a shower. Then he went out.'

'After .... my
new dress, my husband told me that the
taxi had arrived.'

If the two actions are by different people, you have to say who
both the subjects are, and you can't use the . . . *ing* form
of the verb.

3

**'We drove back to the car hire company
and paid the car.'**

To pay someone means *to give money to*. At the car hire company you
pay the man or woman in the office. In a shop you pay
the assistant.

**'We drove back to the car hire company
and .... the car.'**

In this sentence you need a preposition. It is not important
who you give the money to.

4

'My girlfriend has beautiful hairs.'

You talk about *a hair* and the plural *hairs* when you can
count them,
e.g. 'There was a hair in my soup', or worse, 'There were some
hairs in my soup.'

'My girlfriend has beautiful ....'

It's usually difficult to count how many hairs there are on your head, so we use the uncountable form.

5

**'The teacher gave us a paper to write
our compositions on.'**

If you use *a* with paper, it's usually a shorter way of saying
a newspaper,
e.g. 'She went to the shop and bought a bottle of milk and a paper.'

'The teacher gave us .... to
write our compositions on.'

If you want to use *paper* as a countable noun, you have to
use *a piece*. If you want to use it as an uncountable noun, you
don't use the article.

6

'That dress matches you perfectly.'

If one thing matches another thing, it looks good next to it, usually because it is a similar colour or design. You can say that a dress matches your coat or your shoes.

'That dress .... you perfectly.'

If you look good in something you're wearing because it is
the right style for you, you use a different verb.

**'During the last lesson, Annie decided
to make a picture of the class.'**

If you *make* something, it usually means that you build it out
of something,
e.g. 'He made a model of the Sahara desert using sand.'

**'During the last lesson, Annie decided
to .... a picture of the class.'**

You always use another verb for what you do with a camera.

8

'The bank manager said he would be happy
to borrow the money.'

If you borrow something, you *receive* it. A useful reminder is
that if you **B**orrow something, you can **B**ring it home with you.

'The bank manager said he would be happy to .... the money.'

The opposite of *borrow* means that you give something, so it **L**eaves you.

9

'My sister got married with a Chinese man.'

If you got married *with* someone, it would mean that this person married *another* person at the same time as you, e.g. 'Helen got married with her sister.' This is possible, but usually people get married alone.

**'My sister got married .... a
Chinese man.'**

If a woman is talking about her husband, or a man about his
wife, you use *married* with a different preposition. (You also
use the same preposition with *engaged* and *related*.)

10

'Renato is very good in Italian cooking.'

If you use *in* with good, it tells you where a person is good
(or bad, clever, etc.),
e.g. If you say 'Naomi is good in Music', it means
she's good *in the music class* at school.

'Renato is very good ....
Italian cooking.'

If you want to talk about an activity or subject,
e.g. cooking, swimming, art, tennis, you need a
different preposition.

PRACTICE

UNIT THREE

 Decide whether the following sentences are right or wrong. If a sentence is wrong, correct it.

1. Madge has been cleaning thirty windows today.
2. The police have been watching those three men for two hours.
3. Tony has been playing the cello for four hours.
4. Diana has played three piano sonatas by Beethoven this evening.
5. After spending three hours working in the garden, Olwyn went shopping.
6. After cooking a meal with fish in it, my cat Jemima likes licking the plates.
7. After reading a lot of English books, my English became much better.
8. Before we left, Penny went to pay the hotel room.
9. When he comes, can you pay the waiter?
10. Your grandfather's very old, but he has a beautiful hair.
11. Wanda changes the colour of her hairs every month.
12. Can you give me a paper to write Maggie's telephone number on?
13. I don't read much in the week, but I often buy a paper on Sunday.
14. That red skirt really suits your shoes Pat.
15. The new carpet in the living room doesn't match the walls.
16. It's so easy to make pictures with some of the new Japanese cameras.
17. Would you like Mark to take a picture of you?
18. Jack's just going down to the library to lend some books.
19. Do you think you could borrow me your bicycle for the afternoon?
20. I can't play you my favourite cassette because Ege has borrowed it.
21. Honor got married with two of her friends.
22. Maria was engaged with Jimmy for six months before they got married.
23. I didn't know that Paul was married with Holly. I thought they were just good friends.
24. Saraita's class are very good in prepositions.
25. Anthony is very clever at inventing new games.

B *Complete the following text, using one of the words or phrases you have practised in this unit:*

'I'm so tired!' said Mrs Airey, 'I've (make) (1) .... eleven phone calls this morning.' Mrs Airey was busy preparing for her daughter's wedding. Her daughter, Sue, was getting married (2) .... a Frenchman, but the wedding was going to be typically English, in a small village church.

Mrs Airey had (worry) (3) .... all morning – first about the weather. She had heard the weather forecast on the radio and they said it might rain later. Then she had to go to the hairdresser's at 11.00 a.m. to have her (4) .... done. After (5) .... to the hairdresser's, she went round to her neighbour's to (6) .... an umbrella, because she'd lost hers the week before. At 12.00 a.m. she started to get ready. She put on her new green dress and a pair of green shoes that (7) .... it perfectly. She looked very smart, and everyone agreed that green (8) .... her.

After (put on) (9) .... her make-up, Mr Airey arrived. He'd been organizing all the arrangements for getting to the church. 'Have you got the money to (10) .... the taxis?' Mrs Airey asked him.

'Oh no! I forgot!' he replied. 'It's OK, your brother Martin always has lots of cash. He'll (11) .... me the money and I can (12) .... him back on Monday.'

'You're not very good (13) .... remembering things, are you? Did you phone the restaurant to make sure they've got an extra table?' 'No. I didn't forget, but I wrote the phone number on (14) .... paper and I've lost it.'

'Don't worry', said Mrs Airey, noticing how tired he looked. 'I hope you'll be able to smile later, or no one will want to (15) .... a picture of you.'

1

**'I usually read a magazine while I cut
my hair.'**

If you cut your hair it means that you do it *yourself*. Only a
few people cut their own hair, but not while reading a magazine!

'I usually read a magazine while I ....
my hair .... '

For jobs that you get *other* people to do for you, you use the
verb *have* and the Past Participle of the verb. The object
(in this case 'my hair') comes between *have* and the past participle.

2

'We played tennis when it started raining.'

If you use two verbs in the Simple Past with *when*, the verb
after *when* happened first.
It does not matter where *when*
comes in the sentence,
e.g. 'When Jane arrived at the party, everybody gave her a present.'

'We .... tennis when
it started raining.'

Here you need a continuous tense for the action that
started first.

3

'In case the weather gets cold, we'll put our jumpers on.'

If you use *in case*, the verb which comes next is something which *might* happen later. The other verb is something you should do *now* or *before* what might happen, as a preparation or precaution,
e.g. 'You should take some jumpers to England in case the weather is cold.'

'.................. the weather gets cold, we'll
put our jumpers on.'

When you are talking about two actions which both might happen
later, one after the other, you use the normal word
for conditionals.

4

'After her son was convicted of robbery,
Mrs Thomas went to prison to visit him.'

If you go to prison, it means that you're a criminal, and you
have to spend time as a prisoner. If you go to hospital, you
are ill. If you go to university, you are a student.

**'After her son was convicted of robbery,
Mrs Thomas went ....
to visit him.'**

If you are visiting or working in one of these places, but not
receiving the service they give, you need to use an article
before them.

5

**'When few friends arrived at Pat's house,
she decided to have a party.'**

Few means *not enough* or *not many*, so it's often a problem,
e.g. 'Dentists complain that few children clean their teeth
regularly.' If you have *few problems*, that's not many
problems, so it's a good thing.

**'When .... friends arrived at Pat's
house, she decided to have a party.'**

You use the word *few* to mean *some* or *quite a lot* by
using an article with it.

6

**'When Richard got home, the dog was
laying on the sofa.'**

To lay (*laid/has laid*) is always used with an object
after it,
e.g. 'Can you lay the flowers carefully on the table.' When you
are talking about birds like chickens, you can use it without
an object, because everybody understands that they are
laying eggs!

**'When Richard got home, the dog
was .... on the sofa.'**

Here you need the other verb, which can never have an object.

'Paddy always says the truth.'

The truth are not the words used here. Paddy is talking about something that is true, so you use a special expression.

'Paddy always ....'

Because *the truth* are not the words used, but are part of a special expression, you use another verb meaning 'to give information by speaking or writing'.

8

**'At last, I will end my speech by
thanking you for your help.'**

If something happens *at last*, it always means you've been
waiting for it for a long time, longer than you wanted to!
For example, 'We waited for forty minutes. At last, the bus came.'

'.................., I will end my
speech by thanking you for your help.'

If you want to introduce an idea as the last in a list of
ideas, you use another word. This doesn't always mean that
you've been waiting for too long.

9

**'When James goes on holiday, he asks me
to look for his houseplants.'**

If you *look for* something, it is lost and you try to find it.

**'When James goes on holiday, he asks me
to .... his houseplants.'**

Here the meaning is *to keep in good condition* or to *care for*,
but you use *look* with a different preposition.

10

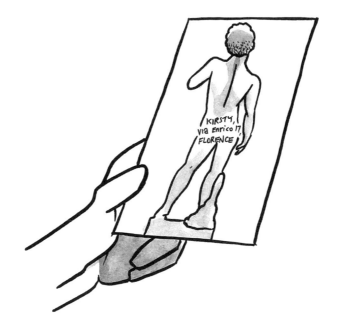

**'Kirsty sent me a postcard of
Michelangelo's *David*, with her
address written on the backside.'**

Backside is a very informal word for your bottom. When English
people complain about someone being lazy, they sometimes say,
'He spends all day sitting on his backside!'

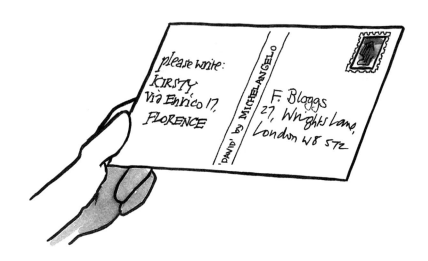

'Kirsty sent me a postcard of
Michelangelo's *David*, with her
address written on the ....'

For the other side of a card, photograph, etc., you use a word
which also describes another part of your body.

PRACTICE

UNIT FOUR

 Say whether the following sentences are right or wrong. If a sentence is wrong, correct it.

1. Satoko is going to the hairdresser's this afternoon to cut her hair.
2. If Gary cuts your hair, he always gives you a drink.
3. I talked and laughed with the passenger sitting next to me when the train crashed.
4. Tony was reading a newspaper when his boss telephoned him.
5. Takuro wrote a letter when all the lights suddenly went out.
6. In case my little brother throws his toys at you, shout at him.
7. Put a swimming costume in your suitcase in case we go to the sea.
8. In case my watch breaks, I'll take it to be repaired.
9. Because Uzi is having problems in class, his parents are going to school next week to talk to the teachers.
10. When you've left school, would you like to go to the university?
11. Tracy's car broke down, so she caught a bus that was going to the prison.
12. It's no problem if you're hungry. Chloe's got a few sandwiches.
13. Richard brought his guitar on the picnic, so we sang few songs and had a really good time.
14. Katherine's very happy with the car – she's had a few problems with it.
15. If you lay the towels out on the grass, they'll dry very quickly.
16. In summer, the park is full of people laying on the grass.
17. If Laila keeps saying lies, no one will ever believe her.
18. Yoshi always tries to tell the truth, even if it's difficult.
19. At last, the rain stopped, and we were able to continue with our walk.
20. Finally, before I end, I'd like to thank Vicki for all the good things she did for me.
21. At last, the important thing I haven't said about prison is that it never succeeds in stopping crime.
22. They still haven't found the gorilla that escaped from London Zoo. The police are looking after it.
23. Could you live in my house and look after the cat while I'm away?
24. I like this photograph of you. Can you sign your name on the backside?
25. I can't remember where I bought that postcard. Is there any writing on the back?

B Complete the following text, using one of the words or phrases you have practised in this unit:

Phillip Marlowe (sleep) (1) .... when the telephone (ring)
(2) .... 'Hello, is that Phillip Marlowe, private detective?', a
voice asked.

'I wish it wasn't,' he replied. 'But to (3) .... the truth, it is.'
There were (4) .... times when he didn't want offers of work,
but this was one of them.

'I wonder if you can help me. Are you busy at the moment?'

'I'm (5) .... in bed at the moment,' Marlowe said. 'In two
hours I'm going to the hairdresser's to (6) ...., but for the rest
of the year I'm not busy.'

'Good. Let me introduce myself. I'm Dirk Phillips, and I'm afraid I've
got (7) .... problems.'

'What are your problems – apart from having a name like Dirk?'

'Well, a friend of mine who sells unusual pets is away on holiday, and she
asked me to look (8) .... her collection of snakes.
Unfortunately one of them has escaped. I think I should find it as soon as
possible (9) .... it bites someone.'

'And why are you asking me to help you?' Marlowe asked.

'Because I've tried everyone else. I (call) (10) .... the police
when I noticed it was missing, but they wouldn't be able to find an
elephant. I've tried the zoo. I even went (11) .... university to
ask someone in the Zoology department to help, but no luck.
(12) .... I decided to try you.'

'Well, I never went (13) .... university – I left school when I
was five. But you want me to look (14) .... your snake. How do
you expect me to find it?'

'I don't know. You're the detective. I'll send you a photograph of the
snake and I'll write my address and phone number on the
(15) .... Give me a call when you find it. Goodbye.'

1

**'After the doctor examined Miss Lavender,
he suggested going to bed.'**

If someone suggests doing something, it means that the speaker
is one of the people who will do it,
e.g. 'I suggest eating outside. We could have a picnic.' It's
the same as saying 'Why don't we ....'

**'After the doctor examined Miss Lavender,
he suggested .... to bed.'**

If you suggest an idea for other people, but not including
yourself, you use *you/he/they* etc., and you don't use the
. . . *ing* form of the verb. Here you can use the Present Simple,
but you mustn't put an *s* on the end of the verb with
he/she/it.

2

'That's Julio. He's coming from Colombia.'

If you use *come* in the continuous form *coming*, it means the action of moving from another place to here.

'That's Julio. He .... from Colombia.'

You must use the simple tense to mean that someone was born in a place.

'Twelve policemen are searching the young boy who went missing yesterday.'

If someone *searches* you, or your room, they examine every part because they think you are hiding something, e.g. 'The customs officer thought I was carrying drugs so he searched me very carefully.'

**'Twelve policemen are ....
the young boy who went missing yesterday.'**

If you use *search* in the same way as *look*, meaning *to try
to find*, you need to use the same preposition too.

4

'We usually have a toast at breakfast time.'

A toast is what you have in a formal situation when everyone lifts their glasses to wish someone success or good health. You can *have*, *drink* or *propose* a toast to someone.

'We usually have .... at
breakfast time.'

What English people eat at breakfast time is
uncountable, so you don't use an article with it. If you want
to make it countable you have to use the word *piece*.

5

**'All our six children are in the bed at
the moment.'**

If you say *the bed*, it means that there is only one,
e.g. 'We all slept on the floor, and Stan slept in the bed.'

'**All our six children are ....
at the moment.**'

Because this is an expression meaning that you are asleep or
haven't got up, you don't use the article.

6

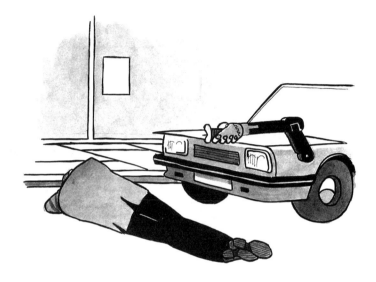

**'A man was badly wounded when a car hit
him in the High Street today.'**

You can be *wounded* in a fight, or in a war, when someone
attacks you with a knife, a gun, or some other weapon. It
means that it breaks through your skin and makes you bleed.

'A man was badly .... when
a car hit him in the High Street today.'

The word you need here can be used for fighting, but can also
be used to describe the damage to your body in an accident.

7

**'Bayern Munich won Liverpool in last
night's football match.'**

If you win something in a competition, it means that it's
given to you to take away as a prize,
e.g. 'Bayern Munich won the European Cup last night',
'Pam won a trip to America in the quiz show.'

**'Bayern Munich .... Liverpool
in last night's football match.'**

You can win the competition, but you need another verb for
what you do to the other people in the competition.

8

**'Edison discovered the record player
in 1876.'**

To discover means *to find*, so you can only discover
something if it's already there, e.g. 'Radium was discovered
by Madame Curie', 'Did Christopher Colombus discover America?'

**'Edison .... the
record player in 1876.'**

Here someone was the first person to *think of* something new
and *make* it.

9

'The policeman was killed by a knife.'

If you use *by* with a passive tense (was killed), it is
followed by the subject of the verb,
e.g. 'The policeman was killed by a criminal'. You can be killed
'by a falling tree', because it's the tree that kills you, not
someone else using the tree in their hands.

**'The policeman was killed ....
a knife.'**

A knife isn't the subject of the verb *to kill*, it's just
the thing which someone used. For the thing which was used you
need a different preposition.

10

**'I nearly forgot to bring the flowers,
but when I saw Belinda she reminded
me of them.'**

If you remind someone *of* something or someone, it usually
means that you have a similar character or appearance, which
makes them think of this thing,
e.g. 'That man with the moustache really reminds me of my
father.' You can also say something which accidentally reminds
someone of something.

**'I nearly forgot to bring the flowers,
but when I saw Belinda she reminded
me .... them.'**

If you remind someone by telling them not to forget something
or asking them about it, it's better to use
another preposition.

PRACTICE

UNIT FIVE

Decide whether the following sentences are right or wrong. If a sentence is wrong, correct it.

1. 'I suggest going by train,' the travel agent said to Sarah.

2. It was so hot that our teacher suggested having a lesson in the garden.

3. 'I suggest getting off at the next stop and walking to the station,' the bus driver said.

4. Can I introduce you to my friend Huang-Mei. She's coming from Taiwan.

5. That was Chris telephoning from the railway station. She's coming up from London to visit us.

6. When Janis speaks, you can hear that she comes from London.

7. When Ron drove into Germany, the customs men searched for his car.

8. Fran couldn't remember where she'd parked her car and spent two hours searching it.

9. When Andrea went to Florence, she spent all day searching for a room.

10. Pam, would you like to have a toast with your coffee?

11. I'd like to propose a toast to John for all the help he's given me.

12. When Norbert was in hospital he had to stay in the bed all day.

13. It was a single room, so I slept on the floor and she slept in the bed.

14. No one died in the plane crash, but many people were wounded.

15. The police caught the robbers, but two policemen were wounded in the fighting.

16. The petrol tanker exploded in the street and thirty-five people were injured.

17. I like playing tennis with Shige, but he often wins me.

18. Keith won a lot of money at the horse races last Saturday.

19. Richard has trained so hard for the race that no one can beat him.

20. It would be really exciting to discover a new planet.

21. I hope you enjoyed the soup. Juliet invented the recipe herself!

22. Anja was hit with a horse that was running away.

23. This lock can only be opened by a very large key.

24. If you see me tomorrow morning, could you remind me of the phone bill?

25. When I hear this music it reminds me of being in Greece.

B *Complete the following text, with one of the words or phrases you have practised in this unit:*

Chris was telling me about his planned trip to Australia in December and I told him that I didn't know what to do at Christmas. 'I suggest (1) .... skiing,' he said, and I laughed. I explained that whenever I heard anything about skiing it reminded me (2) .... a very strange man called Urs, who I met when I was working in Switzerland. He lived in Switzerland and worked for a company that made skis, but he actually (3) .... from Germany. He was crazy about skiing, and every year he entered the men's skiing competition, but he'd never managed to (4) .... it. I saw him working in the factory one day and he told me that he'd (5) .... a new type of ski that could go faster than any other. He was going to try using his new skis in the competition that year and was sure that he could (6) .... the other skiers easily.

Just before the race began, I tried to remind him (7) .... the change they'd made in the race course, but he wasn't listening to me. In fact he went the wrong way and he was going so fast that he disappeared off the side of the mountain! He landed in the forest below and was hit on the head (8) .... one of his skis that came down after him. We spent a couple of hours (9) .... the forest, and there were even mountain dogs (10) .... him in the snow. Eventually we found him, unconscious.

Luckily he wasn't badly (11) .... and we took him home. The doctor examined him and said that he should spend a few days (12) .... bed. I went to visit him and took him a bottle of his favourite whisky. He suggested (have) (13) .... a drink immediately, and soon our glasses were filled (14) .... whisky. 'Let's drink (15) ....,' he said, raising his glass. 'To next year's competition, and an even better type of ski – with brakes!'

ANSWERS

The number in brackets at the end of the practice sentences refers to the page where you will find the grammar explanation.

Unit one

1. Try <u>phoning</u> Michael – he might be at home.
2. There were very <u>few</u> people in the supermarket this morning.
3. After the bell rang, the boxers continued hitting <u>each other</u>.
4. Unfortunately the coffee machine <u>is out of order/out of use</u>.
5. Three men <u>robbed</u> a bank in North London yesterday.
6. The ticket inspector came into the compartment and <u>checked/examined</u> our tickets.
7. My landlady is a very good <u>cook</u>.
8. They hoped the firemen would arrive <u>in time</u>.
9. Nick couldn't reach the hammer, so he asked Bob to throw it <u>to</u> him.
10. Philippa usually goes to work <u>by car</u>. (You can also say 'in her car', but you usually say this when you want to make it clear that it's not another person's car she goes in.)

Practice – 1A

1. WRONG – It's not a difficult thing to do, so he tried <u>knocking</u> on the door. (p. 2)
2. RIGHT. (p. 2)
3. WRONG – It's not easy, so they tried to <u>find</u> it. (p. 1)
4. WRONG – They meet <u>each other</u>. (p. 6)
5. RIGHT. (p. 6)
6. RIGHT. (p. 3)
7. WRONG – There were very <u>few</u> policemen there. (p. 4)
8. RIGHT. (p. 7)
9. WRONG – The lift was <u>out of order</u>. (p. 8)
10. RIGHT. (p. 8)
11. WRONG – The Post Office was <u>robbed</u>. (p. 10)
12. RIGHT. (p. 10)
13. RIGHT. (p. 11)
14. RIGHT. (p. 12)
15. WRONG – The customs men <u>check</u> your luggage. (p. 12)

16. WRONG – She prefers to be the <u>cook</u>. (p. 14)
17. RIGHT. (p. 13)
18. WRONG – The trains never arrive <u>on</u> time (at the scheduled time). (p. 16)
19. WRONG – Vicki didn't turn the taps off <u>in</u> time (to prevent the flood). (p. 16)
20. RIGHT. (p. 15)
21. WRONG – If Harriet wanted to take a photograph, Robert must have been throwing the doll <u>to</u> his little sister. (p. 17)
22. WRONG – Karen threw her tennis racket <u>at</u> Keith (because she was angry). (p. 18)
23. RIGHT – (You shout to someone to get their attention). (p. 18)
24. WRONG – Sue's going to come <u>by</u> bicycle. (p. 19)
25. WRONG – You don't need to go <u>by car</u>. (p. 20)

Practice – 1B

1. by (p. 20)
2. few (p. 4)
3. of order/of use (p. 8)
4. check (p. 12)
5. rob (p. 10)
6. to find (p. 1)
7. little (p. 3)
8. steal (p. 9)
9. on (p. 15)
10. phoning (p. 2)
11. cooks (p. 14)
12. at (p. 17)
13. each other (p. 6)
14. in (p. 16)
15. to (p. 18)

Unit Two

1. I wish you <u>were</u> taller.
2. At work today, my boss told me that I must stop <u>sleeping</u>.

3.   I'm very <u>bored</u> in this class.

4.   Jack had to change <u>trains</u> in Birmingham.

5.   My mother spilt coffee on my dress, <u>so</u> I had to wear a different one.

6.   Your plants have <u>grown</u> a lot since my last visit.

7.   Parents should <u>bring</u> their children <u>up</u> more strictly.

8.   It's nice to go on holiday and be completely <u>carefree</u>.

9.   After two hours, the train arrived <u>at</u> the platform.

10.   My uncle Tom died <u>of</u> pneumonia.

Practice – 2A

1.   RIGHT. (p. 23)

2.   WRONG – Don't you wish I <u>had</u> blue eyes? (p. 24)

3.   WRONG – Diana's friend wishes she <u>would play</u> her music more quietly. (p. 23)

4.   RIGHT. (p. 24)

5.   WRONG – Fiona stopped <u>smoking</u> three years ago. (p. 25)

6.   RIGHT. (p. 25)

7.   WRONG – I stopped <u>learning</u> it when I was fifteen. (p. 26)

8.   WRONG – Tim left before the film finished because he was <u>bored</u>. (p. 28)

9.   WRONG – I'm very <u>excited</u> about my new job, because it's never boring. (p. 28)

10.   WRONG – Because Benedicte did not like the view from the balcony Steve asked if they could change <u>rooms</u>. (p. 30)

11.   RIGHT. (p. 30)

12.   WRONG – The sun shone for five days, <u>so</u> Katie got very brown. (p. 32)

13.   WRONG – The car ran out of petrol, <u>so</u> we had to walk to the hotel. (p. 32)

14.   RIGHT. (p. 32)

15.   WRONG – My dog has <u>grown</u> so much he can jump into the next garden. (p. 34)

16.   RIGHT. (p. 33)

17.   RIGHT. (p. 34)

18.   WRONG – Christine's children are very well <u>brought-up</u>. They never take things without asking. (p. 36)

19. RIGHT. (p. 36)

20. WRONG – My parents <u>brought</u> me <u>up</u> very well and I went to a very good school. (p. 36)

21. WRONG – Miles would like to be young and <u>carefree</u> again. (p. 38)

22. RIGHT. (p. 37)

23. WRONG – There were hundreds of people waiting <u>on</u> the platform when the train arrived. (p. 39)

24. WRONG – The Prime Minister died <u>of</u> a heart attack. (p. 42)

25. RIGHT. (p. 42)

Practice – 2B

1. so (p. 32)

2. on (p. 39)

3. trains (p. 30)

4. would come (p. 23)

5. at (p. 40)

6. shouting (p. 26)

7. hitting (p. 26)

8. bring them up (p. 36)

9. of (p. 42)

10. grown up (p. 33)

11. was/were (p. 24)

12. to let (p. 25)

13. so that (p. 31)

14. bored (p. 28)

15. carefree (p. 38)

Unit Three

1. I <u>have smoked</u> thirty cigarettes today.

2. After I <u>put/I'd put</u> on my new dress, my husband told me that the taxi had arrived.

(It's not <u>necessary</u> to use the Past Perfect (I'd put) with 'after', because this word makes it clear that one past action happened before the next one.)

3. We drove back to the car hire company and <u>paid for</u> the car.

4. My girlfriend has beautiful <u>hair</u>.
5. The teacher gave us <u>a piece of paper/paper/some paper</u> to write our compositions on.
6. That dress <u>suits</u> you perfectly.
7. During the last lesson, Annie decided to <u>take</u> a picture of the class.
8. The bank manager said he would be happy to <u>lend</u> the money.
9. My sister got married <u>to</u> a Chinese man.
10. Renato is very good <u>at</u> Italian cooking.

Practice – 3A

1. WRONG – Madge <u>has cleaned</u> thirty windows today. (p. 45)
2. RIGHT. (p. 45)
3. RIGHT. (p. 45)
4. RIGHT. (p. 46)
5. RIGHT. (p. 47)
6. WRONG – After <u>I cook</u> a meal with fish in it, my cat Jemima likes licking the plates. (p. 47)
7. WRONG – After <u>I read/I had read</u> a lot of English books, my English became much better. (p. 47)
8. WRONG – Before we left, Penny went to <u>pay for</u> the hotel room. (p. 49)
9. RIGHT. (p. 49)
10. WRONG – Your grandfather's very old, but he has beautiful <u>hair</u>. (p. 52)
11. WRONG – Wanda changes the colour of her <u>hair</u> every month. (p. 52)
12. WRONG – Can you give me <u>a piece of paper/some paper</u> to write Maggie's telephone number on? (p. 54)
13. RIGHT. (p. 53)
14. WRONG – That red skirt really <u>matches</u> your shoes Pat. (p. 55)
15. RIGHT. (p. 55)
16. WRONG – It is so easy to <u>take</u> pictures with some of the new Japanese cameras. (p. 58)
17. RIGHT. (p. 58)
18. WRONG – Jack is just going down to the library to <u>borrow</u> some books. (p. 59)

19. WRONG – Do you think you could <u>lend</u> me your bicycle for the afternoon? (p. 60)

20. RIGHT. (p. 59)

21. RIGHT. (p. 61)

22. WRONG – Maria was engaged <u>to</u> Jimmy for six months before they got married. (p. 62)

23. WRONG – I didn't know that Paul was married <u>to</u> Holly. I thought they were just good friends. (p. 62)

24. WRONG – Saraita's class are very good <u>at</u> prepositions. (p. 64)

25. RIGHT. (p. 64)

Practice – 3B

1. made (p. 46)

2. to (p. 62)

3. been worrying (p. 45)

4. hair (p. 52)

5. going/having been (p. 47)

6. borrow (p. 59)

7. matched (p. 55)

8. suited (p. 56)

9. she put on/she'd put on (p. 48)

10. pay for (p. 50)

11. lend (p. 60)

12. pay (p. 49)

13. at (p. 64)

14. a piece of (p. 54)

15. take (p. 58)

Unit Four

1. I usually read a magazine while I <u>have</u> my hair <u>cut</u>.

2. We <u>were playing</u> tennis when it started raining.

3. <u>If</u> the weather gets cold, we'll put our jumpers on.

4. After her son was convicted of robbery, Mrs Thomas went <u>to the prison</u> to visit him.

5. When <u>a few</u> friends arrived at Pat's house, she decided to have a party.

6. When Richard got home, the dog was <u>lying</u> on the sofa. (The verb is to lie/lay/has lain. To lie can also be a regular verb – lied/has lied, meaning 'to not tell the truth'.)

7. Paddy always <u>tells the truth</u>.

8. <u>Finally</u>, I will end my speech by thanking you for your help.

9. When James goes on holiday, he asks me to <u>look after</u> his houseplants.

10. Kirsty sent me a postcard of Michelangelo's *David*, with her address written on the <u>back</u>.

Practice – 4A

1. WRONG – Satoko is going to the hairdresser's this afternoon to <u>have her hair cut</u>. (p. 68)

2. RIGHT. (p. 67)

3. WRONG – I <u>was talking and laughing</u> with the passenger next to me when the train crashed. (p. 70)

4. RIGHT. (p. 70)

5. WRONG – Takuro <u>was writing</u> a letter when all the lights suddenly went out. (p. 70)

6. WRONG – <u>If</u> my little brother throws his toys at you, shout at him. (p. 72)

7. RIGHT. (p. 71)

8. WRONG – *If* my watch breaks, I'll take it to be repaired. (p. 72)

9. WRONG – Because Uzi is having problems in class his parents are going <u>to the school</u> next week to talk to the teachers. (p. 74)

10. WRONG – When you've left school, would you like to go to <u>university</u>? (p. 73)

11. RIGHT. (p. 74)

12. RIGHT. (p. 76)

13. WRONG – Richard brought his guitar on the picnic, so we sang <u>a few</u> songs and had a really good time. (p. 76)

14. WRONG – Katherine's very happy with the car – she's had <u>few</u> problems with it. (p. 75)

15. RIGHT. (p. 77)

16. WRONG – In summer, the park is full of people <u>lying</u> on the grass. (p. 78)

17. WRONG – If Laila keeps <u>telling</u> lies, no one will ever believe her. (p. 80)
18. RIGHT. (p. 80)
19. RIGHT. (p. 81)
20. RIGHT. (p. 82)
21. WRONG – <u>Finally</u>, the important thing I haven't said about prison is that it never succeeds in stopping crime. (p. 82)
22. WRONG – They still haven't found the gorilla that escaped from London Zoo. The police are looking <u>for</u> it. (p. 83)
23. RIGHT. (p. 84)
24. WRONG – I like this photograph of you. Can you sign your name on the <u>back</u>? (p. 86)
25. RIGHT. (p. 86)

Practice – 4B

1. was sleeping (p. 70)
2. rang (p. 70)
3. tell (p. 80)
4. few (p. 75)
5. lying (p. 78)
6. have my hair cut (p. 68)
7. a few (p. 76)
8. after (p. 84)
9. in case (p. 71)
10. called (p. 69)
11. to the (p. 74)
12. Finally (p. 82)
13. to (p. 73)
14. for (p. 83)
15. back (p. 86)

Unit Five

1. After the doctor examined Miss Lavender, he suggested she <u>go</u> to bed. (It is possible to say 'he suggested she <u>went/should go</u> to bed', but some people say that this is not correct English!)

2. That's Julio. He <u>comes</u> from Colombia.
3. Twelve policemen are <u>searching for</u> the boy who went missing yesterday.
4. We usually have <u>toast/a piece of toast</u> at breakfast time.
5. All our six children are <u>in bed</u> at the moment.
6. A man was badly <u>injured</u> when a car hit him in the High Street today.
7. Bayern Munich <u>beat</u> Liverpool in last night's football match.
8. Edison <u>invented</u> the record player in 1876.
9. The policeman was killed <u>with</u> a knife.
10. I nearly forgot to bring the flowers, but when I saw Belinda she reminded me <u>about</u> them.

Practice – 5A

1. WRONG – 'I suggest <u>you go</u> by train,' the travel agent said to Sarah. (p. 90)
2. RIGHT. (p. 89)
3. WRONG – 'I suggest <u>you get</u> off at the next stop and <u>walk</u> to the station,' the bus driver said. (p. 90)
4. WRONG – Can I introduce you to my friend Huang-Mei. She <u>comes</u> from Taiwan. (p. 92)
5. RIGHT. (p. 91)
6. RIGHT. (p. 92)
7. WRONG – When Ron drove into Germany, the customs men <u>searched</u> his car. (p. 93)
8. WRONG – Fran couldn't remember where she'd parked her car and spent two hours <u>searching for it</u>. (p. 94)
9. RIGHT. (p. 94)
10. WRONG – Pam, would you like to have <u>toast/a piece of toast</u> with your coffee? (p. 96)
11. RIGHT. (p. 95)
12. WRONG – When Norbert was in hospital he had to stay <u>in bed</u> all day. (p. 98)
13. RIGHT. (p. 97)
14. WRONG – No one died in the plane crash, but many people were <u>injured</u>. (p. 100)

15. RIGHT. (p. 99)

16. RIGHT. (p. 100)

17. WRONG – I like playing tennis with Shige, but he often <u>beats</u> me. (p. 102)

18. RIGHT. (p. 101)

19. RIGHT. (p. 102)

20. RIGHT. (p. 104)

21. RIGHT. (p. 103)

22. WRONG – Anja was hit <u>by</u> a horse that was running away. (p. 105)

23. WRONG – This lock can only be opened <u>with</u> a very large key. (p. 106)

24. WRONG – If you see me tomorrow morning, could you remind me <u>about</u> the phone bill? (p. 108)

25. RIGHT. (p. 107)

Practice – 5B

1. you go (p. 90)

2. of (p. 107)

3. came (p. 92)

4. win (p. 102)

5. invented (p. 103)

6. beat (p. 102)

7. about (p. 108)

8. by (p. 105)

9. searching (p. 93)

10. searching for (p. 94)

11. injured (p. 100)

12. in (p. 98)

13. having (p. 89)

14. with (p. 106)

15. a toast (p. 95)